The 50 Most
TERRIFYING
Roller Coasters
Ever Built

Nick Weisenl

D1417659

Copyright Information

Second Edition – Paperback Version
Copyright ©2015 by Nick Weisenberger

ISBN-13: 978-1500699963
ISBN-10: 1500699969

Dedicated to Henry. Ride on son.

Your Free Bonus

As a way of saying thanks for your purchase, I'm offering a free bonus gift that's exclusive to my book and blog readers.

Theme parks and roller coasters are fun – waiting in long lines is not. If you want to save precious time during your amusement park visit you'll need to steer clear of those long queues. I've included my best advice to avoid wasting hours of your day by standing in line for one of the most terrifying roller coasters this summer in an action-packed pdf. You can download this free resource at:

http://www.thrillingbooks.net/FREE

Table of Contents

Introduction

The world's coaster count is rapidly approaching three thousand operating scream machines that give hundreds of millions of safe rides every year. What makes these thrill rides so addicting? The experience of controlled falling is scary, but also exhilarating. The appearance of danger through speed and sensation provide an incredible adrenaline rush. Coaster enthusiasts strap themselves into these scream machines simply because they love being scared in a safe environment. The sensation of weightlessness or the simulated experience of being thrown from the train reinforces the feeling of danger. No, roller coasters are not dreamt up by an evil genius, designed with the sole purpose of scaring patrons to death. Roller coaster engineers make the riders feel extreme forces while keeping them safe and secure.

Some roller coasters are more terrifying than others. Of course, coasters towering taller than a certain height are terrifying for many individuals, but it would be boring to simply make a list of the world's tallest coasters. As a result, most of the bone-chilling machines in this countdown do not use sheer height to terrify, but instead prey on our fears and emotions in other more creative ways. One element alone may not make a ride terrifying, but the sum of all of its parts does. What factors make a ride terrifying? Height, speed, inversions, backwards segments, unique track elements, darkness, and unexpected surprises all contribute to making your head spin and your knees tremble.

Terminology

Before we get into the list of the most terrifying roller coasters, there is terminology to become familiar with so we can speak in "coaster talk," if you will. You see, coaster enthusiasts love to give everything a name, from the type of vehicles to the way the track is twisted to how tall the ride is. It all has a term or name.

Coaster Type: Wood or Steel

Every roller coaster is classified as being one of two types: wooden or steel. According to the Roller Coaster Database (http://www.rcdb.com), there are approximately 2,800 roller coasters operating worldwide today. Of these, only 172 (or 6.14%) are classified as "wood" coasters. The difference is primarily based on the material that the rails are constructed from, and not what the supports are made of. Generally, steel roller coasters are defined as a roller coaster with track consisting of tubular steel rails, while wooden coaster tracks are made from layers of laminated wood. Technically speaking, every wooden roller coaster is actually a "steel" coaster because all the wheels ride on bands of steel. This track steel sits on top of a stack of eight pieces of wood, "the stack" being what defines it as a true wooden coaster. The top two pieces of wood are wider than the stack they sit on so the safety or up-stop wheels can run below them, thus preventing the vehicles from leaving the track. In the future, these two types may not exist, as the line between them has become more and more blurred.

Seating Configurations

Pretty much any and every seating arrangement or configuration that you can think of for a roller coaster has been attempted somewhere in the world. Seats can be above the track, below the track, or to the side of the track. They can also be fixed or able to spin freely. Named variations include:

4th dimension: Controlled rotatable seats cantilevered on each side of the track.

Bobsled: Cars travel freely down a U-shaped track (no rails) like a bobsled, except on wheels.

Floorless: The vehicle sits above the track but contains no floor between the riders' feet and the rails, allowing their legs to dangle freely.

Inverted: Vehicle is fixed below the rails with riders' feet hanging freely, and is able to invert upside down.

Laydown/flying: Riders are parallel to the rails, either on their backs or stomachs.

Motorbike: Riders straddle the seats as if riding motorcycles, jet skis, or horses.

Sit down: Traditional roller coaster with vehicles above the rails.

Spinning: Seats can freely spin on a horizontal axis.

Stand-up: Riders are restrained in a standing position.

Swinging suspended: The vehicle hangs below the rails and can freely swing from side to side but does not invert.

Pipeline: Riders are positioned between the rails instead of above or below them.

Wingrider: The seats are fixed on both sides of the vehicle outside of the rails.

Coaster Class

Roller coasters that fall into a specific height range are referred to as one of the terms below. Interestingly, rides of a certain height have a name, but rides of a certain length do not (not yet anyway).

* ❖ Hyper: 200–299 feet tall
* ❖ Giga: 300–399 feet tall
* ❖ Strata: 400–499 feet tall

Inversions and Other Terminology

Airtime: Roller coasters can thrust negative Gs on riders, causing them to momentarily lift off their seats and become "weightless." As the vehicle flies over the top of a hill the load on the passenger becomes less than Earth's gravity and, in the extreme, could throw an unrestrained passenger out of the car. Scream machines with oodles of so-called "airtime" moments or "butterflies in your stomach" thrills rank among the world's best. Negative g-forces cannot be too great because, when under high negative g-forces, blood rushes to the head and can cause "red out."

Cobra roll: A half-loop followed by half a corkscrew, then another half corkscrew into another half-loop. The trains are inverted twice and exit the element in the opposite direction from which they entered.

A cobra roll inversion

Corkscrew: A loop where the entrance and exit points have been stretched apart.

A corkscrew or flatspin

Dive loop: The track twists upward and to the side, similar to half a corkscrew, before diving towards the ground in a half-loop. Basically this is the opposite of an Immelman inversion.

G force: G-force is expressed as a ratio of the force developed in changing speed or direction relative to the force felt due to the Earth's gravity. The smaller the curve radius and the higher the speed, the greater the g-force felt. Thus, a 2g force on a 100-pound body causes it to weigh 200 pounds (weight = mass x g-force). Indianapolis 500 racers are subjected to more than 3 Gs in the corners of their hairpin turns, while there are looping coasters that subject passengers to as much as 6 Gs. Positive g-forces, meaning those that push your butt into the seat, become uncomfortable for the human body at +5 G and may cause the loss of consciousness.

Immelman: Named after the aircraft maneuver pioneered by Max Immelman, the inversion begins with a vertical loop but, at the apex of the inversion, turns into a corkscrew, exiting at the side instead of completing the loop. This is the opposite of a dive loop element.

About the List

This list is based upon the opinions of the author and not grounded in any scientific research. Coasters are ranked in reverse order, from 50 to 1, with 1 being the most terrifying or extreme. Every ride includes pertinent information and stats, such as name, location, height, inversions, etc., as well as an explanation for why it made this list.

If you visit multiple Six Flags parks (as an example), you may notice that some of the coasters are very similar, and in some cases may be exactly the same. Many roller coasters are "clones" or copies of the same ride. If two rides are very similar, I've decided to only list one of them. For example, Top Thrill Dragster was built first, but Kingda Ka is taller and faster, which is why I have included it and omitted Dragster. As another example, Maurer has built several SkyLoop models, but I have chosen the one with a few additional elements (called Abismo). Also please note roller coasters due to open in 2015 and beyond have not been included in this list.

Spoiler Alert: One of the most terrifying aspects of any ride is the element of surprise. If you continue reading the thrill of the attractions may be spoiled for you as each ride listed contains a description of the elements that make it terrifying and unique. Finally, onto the countdown…

The Fifty Most Terrifying Roller Coasters Ever Built...

50. HOLLYWOOD RIP RIDE ROCKIT

Known for: World's first track elements
Park: Universal Studios Florida
Location: United States
Type: Steel
Opened: 2009
Designer/Manufacturer: Maurer Söhne
Height (ft.): 167
Speed (mph): 65
Video: http://youtu.be/Jjl2a8wRe34

Hollywood Rip Ride Rockit is a radically innovative steel coaster that includes one-of-a-kind track elements, cutting-edge technology, and an interactive audio element. Sprawling across a large section of the park, the skyline of Universal Studios Florida was changed forever when the Rockit began thrilling in August of 2009. Riders board a train consisting of two six-passenger cars before ascending the 167-foot-tall vertical lift hill. After reaching a speed of 65 mph, the ride soars into a mammoth non-inverting loop (a loop that twists at the top so the vehicles never turn upside down). This crazy maneuver is followed by the Treble Clef (where guests burst through a building façade on track shaped like the music symbol), and later followed by the Jump Cut, a spiraling, negative-gravity move. If nothing else, Hollywood Rip Ride Rockit is surely one of the coolest looking coasters around, especially at night when the lights on the vehicles are lit up.

The most unique aspect of Hollywood Rip Ride Rockit is the ability to choose your own song to rock out to. That is, if you can hear it over your own screaming. The music selection is broken up into 30 songs in five categories: Classic Rock/Heavy Metal, Club/Electronica, Country, Rap/Hip-Hop, and Pop Music/Disco. In addition to these 30 songs, Universal has also included a number of "hidden" tracks that are accessible via entering secret codes into the ride's touchpads before your journey begins. A personalized take-home music video is also available for purchase for those wanting to remember and share their terrifying ordeal with their friends.

49. ABYSS

Known for: Underwear dispensers
Park: Adventure World
Location: Australia
Type: Steel
Opened: 2013
Designer/Manufacturer: Gerstlauer Amusement Rides GmbH
Height (ft.): 98.4
Drop (ft.): 100
Speed (mph): 52.8
Inversions: 3
Video: http://www.youtube.com/watch?v=rCfoMj4gdZE

Australia's Adventure World opened Abyss in 2013, a custom-designed Gerstlauer Euro-Fighter coaster (the first of its kind in the country). Riders of the $12 million coaster board one of four trains seating eight passengers each. The journey begins inside a dark show building where the vehicles navigate a few twists and turns before rolling riders upside down through an inline twist in the dark. Then it's outside and up the 100-foot-tall vertical lift hill. The beyond vertical first drop sends the cars zipping along in excess of 52 mph during the ride's 2,066-foot-long course. A dive loop and Immelman loop complete the inversion count before the vehicles return to the station inside the show building.

In an effort to help promote Abyss as Australia's most terrifying coaster, the park placed underwear dispensers outside the exit of the ride, stocked with packets of fresh clean white underpants. Along with the "tighty whities," the undies packets contain a fact sheet outlining all of the key statistics and features relating to the ride. The park hasn't revealed how many guests have actually needed the packets.

48. The RATTLER

Known for: World's largest wood coaster when it debuted
Park: Six Flags Fiesta Texas
Location: United States
Type: Wood
Opened: 1992
Closed: 2012
Designer/Manufacturer: John Pierce
Height (ft.): 179.7
Drop (ft.): 124
Speed (mph): 65
Video: http://youtu.be/BPXBkuN-O18

When the Rattler opened at Six Flags Fiesta Texas in 1992, it was the tallest and fastest wooden coaster in the world. The lift hill climbed to an impressive height of 179 feet, followed by a gut-wrenching drop of 166 feet at a blistering speed of 73 mph. Adding to the ride's excitement was its incredible location, situated on top of, next to, and even carved through a rock quarry wall. Unfortunately, the coaster's original plans never called for such a large first drop. The construction of the 161-foot-tall Mean Streak at Cedar Point prompted the park to alter the design at the last minute in order to make it the record holder. The hasty changes negatively affected the layout due to very rough transitions between elements, resulting in many riders complaining of rib or back pain. The park was subsequently forced to make modifications to the ride, and shortened the first drop from 166 to 124 feet, resulting in a reduction of its top speed from 73 to 65 mph.

There's a saying about wooden roller coasters: "If it doesn't shake, it's going to break." Wooden roller coaster structures are designed to sway a couple of inches as the train goes racing by, especially in tight corners and high g-force sections. Think of it like this: When you jump off of a tall object, you land safely by allowing your legs to flex and bend at the knee. Otherwise, if you kept your legs straight, you might shatter your leg bone or bust your knee joint. This same basic principle applies to a wooden roller coaster. The structure must be allowed to give and flex like a shock absorber in order to keep it from internally shaking itself to pieces. The Rattler was notorious for how much the structure would sway as the train raced by. See for yourself in this video: (http://youtu.be/sLfQBW9wnDI).

The Rattler was closed in 2012 to be transformed into the Iron Rattler steel coaster.

47. RIDDLER'S REVENGE

Known for: World's largest stand-up coaster
Park: Six Flags Magic Mountain
Location: United States
Type: Steel
Opened: 1998
Designer/Manufacturer: Bolliger & Mabillard
Height (ft.): 156
Drop (ft.): 146
Speed (mph): 65
Inversions: 6
Video: http://www.youtube.com/watch?v=WrsvkjhSwEQ

When Riddler's Revenge opened in 1998, it became the world recorder holder in height, drop, speed, length, and number of inversions for a stand-up roller coaster. Instead of sitting in a seated position, riders stand up while hurtling through massive inversions, including two back-to-back dive loops. Riders straddle small bicycle-style seats, meaning this coaster may be slightly more terrifying for males than females, especially if they dream of having children in the future.

Between 1982 and 1999, only twenty-one stand-up

roller coasters were built. Of these, Bolliger & Mabillard (B&M) created seven of their own, and Riddler's Revenge remains the cream of the crop.

46. THE BAT

Known for: World's first suspended coaster
Park: Kings Island
Location: United States
Type: Steel
Opened: 1993
Designer/Manufacturer: Arrow Dynamics
Height (ft.): 78
Drop (ft.): 70
Speed (mph): 51
Video: http://www.youtube.com/watch?v=Sg-OWKFyp8A

One of the most notorious rides in roller coaster history is The Bat at Kings Island. It was the first-ever suspended roller coaster, where the cars hang below the rails and are free to swing freely from side to side. The Bat only operated sporadically between 1981 and 1983 before being dismantled in 1985. Over the years, the legend of the Bat has grown due to the outrageous rumors about why the ride was destroyed, and because so few people were able to ride it. Contrary to many wild stories, the Bat never killed or even injured a rider. Poor engineering of the trains, track, and structure is what really lead to the ride's demise. A year after the Bat was removed, the Vortex looping coaster was erected in the Bat's place, and actually reused the station. Concrete footers from the Bat can still be seen beneath the Vortex's structure. The suspended roller coaster returned to Kings Island in 1993 with the addition of Top Gun (renamed Flight Deck, and later re-themed as The Bat). If you were fortunate enough to ride the original Bat, consider yourself lucky!

45. FURIUS BACO

Known for: World's first launched wingrider
Park: Port Adventura
Location: Spain
Type: Steel
Opened: 2007
Designer/Manufacturer: Intamin AG
Height (ft.): 46
Speed (mph): 83.9
Inversions: 1
Video: http://www.youtube.com/watch?v=Lpl1zlq9jXY

Furius Baco was the world's first wing coaster where the seats are cantilevered off the side of the train instead of being on top of or below the rails, allowing passengers' feet to dangle freely. What makes Furius Baco even more unique is that it's the world's only launched wing coaster. While many other launched rides launch immediately into a giant hill, Furius Baco races off of the launch track and dips down into a trench. Because the wingspan of the vehicles is so wide, the outside seats are far away from the center of gravity of the trains and often result in a rough and bumpy ride. This could be one of the reasons why Furius Baco has been the only wingrider with stationary seats sold and manufactured by Intamin. The wingrider market is now dominated by B&M, who appear to have solved the roughness problem and also just launched their first launched wingrider, Thunderbird at Holiday World.

44. SAW: THE RIDE

Known for: Horror movie themed coaster
Park: Thorpe Park
Location: United Kingdom
Type: Steel
Opened: 2009
Designer/Manufacturer: Gerstlauer Amusement Rides GmbH
Height (ft.): 100
Drop (ft.): 99.5
Speed (mph): 55
Inversions: 3
Video: http://www.youtube.com/watch?v=t0_Sk4uDhEo

The world's first horror movie themed roller coaster opened at Thorpe Park in 2009. Saw: The Ride begins in the Jigsaw Killer's booby-trapped warehouse where riders board a two-car, eight-passenger train. The nightmare begins by twisting slowly through the darkness. The first trap encountered is a pair of swinging axes and metal spikes. At the last second the car plunges down an unseen, nearly vertical drop, giving riders a jolt of airtime. The car levels and slows along a straight section of track as air cannons are blasted at riders, giving the effect of deadly crossbows firing over their heads. Just when they've think they have escaped, the track spirals into a barrel roll. As the cars are hanging upside down, a body is seen lying on the floor directly below in a pool of blood, and it suddenly squirts "blood" (water) at the victims in the train. The vehicles exit the building and travel towards the 100-foot-tall vertical lift hill. As the cars climb towards the heaven, it becomes clear that the ride is only half over, as two more inversions await.

43. HADES 360

Known for: Longest underground tunnel
Park: Mt. Olympus Water & Theme Park
Location: United States
Type: Wood
Opened: 2005
Designer/Manufacturer: The Gravity Group, LLC
Height (ft.): 136
Drop (ft.): 140
Speed (mph): 60
Inversions: 1
Video: http://youtu.be/xFhj4mVWCSY

Hades 360 at Mount Olympus Theme Park in Wisconsin Dells, Wisconsin, is the only traditional track wooden roller coaster to go upside down. This twisted coaster actually opened sans inversion as Hades in 2005. In 2013, it was renovated by the original designers, the Gravity Group, to add a corkscrew inversion (a 110-degree overbanked turn) and new state-of-the-art trains.

Unsuspecting riders are surprised to discover that the most terrifying feature of the ride isn't the inversion—it's the

800 feet of underground tunnel, the world's longest on a coaster. The trains plummet down the 140-foot drop into complete darkness as they travel under the park's parking lot, experiencing many dips and twists and a ninety-degree banked turn before emerging back into daylight, only to find themselves upside down. Without pausing even for a second, the action continues as the trains plunge back underground to travel under the parking lot again. The trains emerge into daylight once more and fly into a tall camel back next to the lift hill that has riders wondering if the coaster breaks the laws of physics. How the trains have enough momentum to make it over a few more airtime hills and helix after all that is a mystery, but one thing we know for sure is that it's certainly a terrifying ride!

42. REVENGE OF THE MUMMY: THE RIDE

Known for: False ending
Park: Universal Studios Florida
Location: United States
Type: Steel
Opened: 2004
Designer/Manufacturer: Premier Rides
Height (ft.): 45
Drop (ft.): 25
Speed (mph): 45
Video: http://www.youtube.com/watch?v=ydJ1M13rRYE

Revenge of the Mummy: The Ride combines a high adrenaline indoor coaster with show elements and special effects based on Universal Studios' *Mummy* trilogy. Opened in 2004 as a replacement for the Kongfrontation dark ride that closed in 2002, this 2,200-foot-long coaster contains two launch sequences and a short section in which the 16-seat "mine car" travels backwards. Riders come face-to-face with the mummies themselves as they navigate through an Egyptian tomb. The coaster spawned two other "Revenge of the Mummy" coasters — one at Universal Studios Hollywood (opened June 2004) and the other at Universal Studios Singapore (opened 2010).

Perhaps the most memorable moment of the attraction is the false ending. Midway through the ride the mine car comes screeching to a halt, and it appears that the ride is over. There's a shadow of a ride op in a control booth to the left, but all of a sudden lights below the window begin to flash, the glass of the booth breaks, and big baddie Imhotep appears. "Prepare to forfeit your souls," he warns, and the ceiling bursts into flames! The room heats up fast as the mummy screams "Death is only the beginning!" and you're launched down an extremely surprising drop into a misty pit where your picture is taken. Now you can remember this terrifying moment for all time!

41. NEMESIS

Known for: Majority of the track is below ground
Park: Alton Towers
Location: United Kingdom
Type: Steel
Opened: 1994
Designer/Manufacturer: Bolliger & Mabillard
Height (ft.): 42.7
Drop (ft.): 104
Speed (mph): 50
Inversions: 4
Video: http://www.youtube.com/watch?v=SYsw99YKHLw

Alton Towers in the United Kingdom has the unique challenge of not being allowed to build any rides taller than the tree line. Initially, this restriction might seem like it would  result in some pretty lame coaster designs. In fact, just the opposite is true! It forces the designers to be more creative, as was the case with Nemesis, Europe's first inverted roller coaster. The ride's concept was created by John Wardley and was manufactured by B&M. To make up for the fact that they weren't able to go very high, the designers decided to do the opposite and go down. Much of the coaster resides in trenches and tunnels, while rivers of "blood" flow down the sides. Nemesis is considered to be one of the best inverted coasters ever built, and even spawned a "sequel," Nemesis Inferno at Thorpe Park.

40. ALPENGEIST

Known for: Tallest inverted coaster
Park: Busch Gardens Williamsburg
Location: United States
Type: Steel
Opened: 1997
Designer/Manufacturer: Bolliger & Mabillard
Height (ft.): 195
Drop (ft.): 170
Speed (mph): 67
Inversions: 6
Video: http://www.youtube.com/watch?v=_cf5SxtCP4o

Alpengeist at Busch Gardens Williamsburg is themed to the legendary snow beast of the Alps and translates as "Ghost of the Alps" in German. This coaster was designed and built by B&M out of Monthey, Switzerland, and opened on March 22, 1997. The lift hill is themed to a ski lift and tops out as the tallest inverted roller coaster in the world. It also has the longest drop of any inverted coaster and a maximum speed of 67 mph.

While other inverted coasters feature compact layouts with tight inversions, Alpengeist is known for its huge, drawn out loops and meandering, terrain-hugging layout. Coaster enthusiasts say it lacks the snappiness of the smaller inverts but nevertheless, the sheer speed in the low points is terrifying. And you can't deny the beauty of the most iconic element of the ride - the colossal cobra roll situated over the majestic Rhine River.

39. MYSTERY MINE

Known for: Cliffhanger element
Park: Dollywood
Location: United States
Type: Steel
Opened: 2007
Designer/Manufacturer: Gerstlauer Amusement Rides GmbH
Speed (mph): 46
Inversions: 2
Video: http://youtu.be/Ef5xgK2OQXQ

What if there is no light at the end of the tunnel? That's the question posed to riders at Dollywood's Mystery Mine steel coaster. In total, 1,811 feet of twisting track travels around and through an abandoned coal mine. The ride doesn't waste any time in getting started, plunging down a drop into the dark immediately upon exiting the station. Next up is an underbanked turn where the track is banked to the outside instead of the inside of the curve. After passing an ominous room full of ravens, the cars duck under a massive, spinning rock crusher before coming to the first vertical lift, which leads outside of the mine. The cars then cruise through some drops and helixes before re-entering the mine and climbing another vertical lift, this one the taller of the two.

At the apex of the lift the cars stall and riders see boxes of dynamite stacked high. A fuse is lit and snakes its way toward the boxes. Just as flames begin to shoot out, the cars plummet down a 95-degree drop that has a slight rotation to the right at the same time. The cars speed out into daylight to encounter a rapid-fire barrel roll followed by another half roll. The vehicles slow to a crawl, almost to a stop, as the riders experience hang time with nothing holding them in except the shoulder harnesses. Just when it seems they are about to get stuck, the cars complete a half-loop into the brake run.

38. MAGNUM XL-200

Known for: First coaster to break 200 feet
Park: Cedar Point
Location: United States
Type: Steel
Opened: 1989
Designer/Manufacturer: Arrow Dynamics
Height (ft.): 205
Drop (ft.): 194.7
Speed (mph): 72
Video: http://www.youtube.com/watch?v=EmW1BirrgsY

Magnum XL-200 opened in 1989 and was the first roller coaster to break the 200-foot-tall mark. Interestingly, a 1989 park brochure listed the ride's height at only 201 feet tall, versus the 205-foot-tall statistic seen today. The 201-foot statistic came from the ride's blueprints and did not account for the height of the footers (the cement foundations that stick out of the ground) the coaster sits on. The Magnum is a traditional "out and back" coaster featuring 5,106 feet of track that winds its way over the neighboring Soak City waterpark and along the shores of Lake Erie, giving riders a breathtaking view. This is easily one of the best locations of any coaster in existence.

In 2006, the Magnum XL-200 was voted number three in the "Best Steel Roller Coaster in the World" category in a poll conducted by *Amusement Today*. Since 1989, Magnum has given more than 36 million guests a ride to remember. In 2006 alone, 1,826,338 guests rode Magnum. Riders must be at least 48 inches tall. As impressive as the numbers are, coaster enthusiasts will tell you that the element that makes Magnum truly terrifying is its airtime, that incredible feeling of floating over each of the ride's intense bunny hills.

37. TOWER OF TERROR

Known for: Extreme g-forces
Park: Gold Reef City
Location: South Africa
Type: Steel
Opened: 2001
Designer/Manufacturer: Ronald Bussink
Height (ft.): 111.6
Drop (ft.): 164.1
Speed (mph): 59
Video: http://www.youtube.com/watch?v=ICyfbZ1-qJU

Tower of Terror is a sit-down roller coaster located at Gold Reef City in Gauting, South Africa. Designed by Nauta-Bussink and manufactured by local companies, this coaster was originally built with a 45-degree lift hill that was later replaced with an elevator-style lift system. After ascending the lift, the mine cars are pushed slowly towards the twisted vertical drop. The cars plummet over the edge and fall 164 feet, 49 of which are in an underground former mine shaft. The pullout of the drop is so sharp that it subjects riders to 6.3 Gs, the highest g-force on any roller coaster in the world. In comparison, Indianapolis 500 racers are subjected to more than 3 Gs in the corners of their hairpin turns. When humans are under high positive Gs, blood is forced from the head to the feet, eventually causing a "grey out." If there were a way to quantify this, Tower of Terror might take the record for most intensity per foot of track of any coaster in the world.

36. VOLCANO

Known for: Inverted launch coaster
Park: Kings Dominion
Location: United States
Type: Steel
Opened: 1998
Designer/Manufacturer: Intamin AG
Height (ft.): 155
Drop (ft.): 80
Speed (mph): 70
Inversions: 4
Video: http://www.youtube.com/watch?v=Nm7NRZ0BVWE

Volcano: The Blast Coaster at Kings Dominion is the world's first inverted roller coaster to feature a linear induction motor (LIM) launch, and is the only one of its kind that completes a full circuit. Paramount (the original owners of the park at the time) wanted to redevelop what used to be home to a log flume and boat ride, but without removing the iconic mountain. The idea was hatched to have a coaster come shooting out of the center of the mountain. Volcano was born!

The coaster was built by Intamin AG and opened on August 13, 1998, with four inversions, a length of 2,757 feet, a height of 155 feet, a drop of 80 feet, and a top speed of 70 mph. After launching into a large helix, the trains hit a surprising second launch inside the volcano that blasts them straight up and out the top! You're immediately flipped upside down before spiraling around the mountain and through three inline twists, then plunging back into the volcano and into the station. Did that just happen?

35. HIGH ROLLER

Known for: Built on top of a tower
Park: Stratosphere Tower
Location: United States
Type: Steel
Opened: 1996
Closed: 2005
Designer/Manufacturer: Premier Rides
Drop (ft.): 20
Speed (mph): 30
Video: http://www.youtube.com/watch?v=OgswFsHIkeg

Compared to the other scream machines on this list, the High Roller isn't much more than a kiddie coaster, with its small drop, relatively slow speed, and uninspiring layout. What makes it terrifying is its placement on top of the 1149-foot-tall Stratosphere Tower. The High Roller's bright red track wraps around the tower at the 909-foot mark, level 12A, making it the highest coaster ever. . The ride itself consisted of loops around the Stratosphere tower, slowly descending, and then ascending again for a second revolution. Riding in the outer seat, the one closest to the edge of the building, was a truly frightening experience.

However, since it was connected to the tower, it couldn't go too fast without risking the integrity of the building. Shut downs due to high winds were very frequent. High Roller closed in 2005 to make way for newer cutting-edge attractions on top of the tower that may be even more terrifying than High Roller was.

34. THE BEAST

Known for: World's longest wooden coaster
Park: Kings Island
Location: United States
Type: Wood
Opened: 1979
Designer/Manufacturer: Charlie Dinn
Height (ft.): 110
Drop (ft.): 141
Speed (mph): 64.8
Video: http://www.youtube.com/watch?v=ZJuhNpWMfdE

The Beast opened on April 14, 1979, as the tallest, fastest, and longest wooden roller coaster in the world, and has more than lived up to its name. This monstrosity is still the longest wooden roller coaster in the world, lasting more than four minutes and sprawling over 35 densely wooded acres on the outskirts of Kings Island. The Beast originally featured three underground tunnels. By its second season, the second and third underground tunnels had been combined into one longer one so that an access road could be built. While legendary during the daytime, the Beast becomes an absolutely terrifying experience after nightfall. The number of tunnels suddenly becomes irrelevant as the darkness of the forest makes it impossible to determine when you're underground and when you're simply under the trees.

33. LEVIATHAN

Known for: B&M's first giga coaster
Park: Canada's Wonderland
Location: Canada
Type: Steel
Opened: 2012
Designer/Manufacturer: Bolliger & Mabillard
Height (ft.): 306
Drop (ft.): 306
Speed (mph): 92
Video: http://youtu.be/lpJsEamxUSQ

Leviathan is the 306-foot-tall giga coaster at Canada's Wonderland that debuted in 2012. The first drop is huge, the speed is maintained throughout, and it's so comfortable you could ride it all day long. The first drop plunges the 32 passenger cars down an 80-degree drop at 92 mph, straight into a tunnel. The tallest and fastest roller coaster in Canada, Leviathan is also the tallest roller coaster built by the world-renowned Bolliger and Mabillard. In fact, it's only the third non-launched 300-foot-tall giga coaster built in North America (behind Millennium Force and Intimidator 305, both built by Intamin). Leviathan was a $28 million investment, coming in at a total length of 5,486 feet. It resides in the Medieval Faire section of the park and is themed to a mythical sea creature. Leviathan uses the standard four-across seating found on most B&M coasters, and not the staggered V-type seating seen on its little brother, Behemoth. Another interesting fact is that it's the seventh tallest and eighth fastest roller coaster in the world.

32. DUELING DRAGONS

Known for: Near-miss collision elements
Park: Islands of Adventure
Location: Dueling Dragons
Type: Steel
Opened: 1999
Designer/Manufacturer: Bolliger & Mabillard
Height (ft.): 125
Drop (ft.): 115
Speed (mph): 60
Inversions: 5
Video: http://www.youtube.com/watch?v=hKdw2mf_8Lo

Dueling Dragons is actually two roller coasters, a pair of intertwined inverts that "duel." Dueling roller coasters offer a thrilling element not typically found on single-track rides: the near-miss collision. Two trains travel directly toward one another, often at a combined speed in excess of 100 mph, seemingly on a head-on collision course — only to veer away at the last breathtaking second, narrowly avoiding the other train by a few inches.

How is the dueling effect achieved? The main variable to compensate for is weight. But how do you weigh a fully loaded coaster train? The solution is actually pretty simple. The weight of the trains can be determined by measuring the current draw on the lift hill motors (or LIMs, in the case of a launched ride). This can be done because the weight of the loaded train is directly proportional to the power needed to pull the train up the lift hill. For example, say you know the weight of an empty train. You can measure the current draw on the motor as the train proceeds up the lift. Next, add a few water dummies with a known weight to the train and take another current measurement. Now we can interpolate between those numbers in order to determine other unknown weights using the current draw alone.

On June 18, 2010, Dueling Dragons was officially rebranded as Dragon Challenge in conjunction with the opening of The Wizarding World of Harry Potter at Universal's Island of Adventure. On October 19, 2011, it was announced that this coaster will no longer "duel" and is instead being billed as a "high-speed chase between two coasters." For safety reasons, the trains will no longer be sent out together and the near misses will no longer occur (which is why it's listed as Dueling Dragons and not the duel-less Dragon Challenge).

31. WICKED

Known for: Horizontal and vertical launch
Park: Lagoon Park
Location: United States
Type: Steel
Opened: 2007
Designer/Manufacturer: Zierer
Height (ft.): 110
Speed (mph): 55
Inversions: 1
Video: http://youtu.be/HcLZn1vSGso

The star attraction of Lagoon Park is Wicked, the LSM tower launch coaster. Wicked was designed in house by Lagoon's engineers and manufactured by Zierer. The ride cost $10 million to build, and nearly 1.5 million of that was just for the sixty-foot-deep pilings and foundations. Wicked features a unique observation window into the control system room from the queue line. The trains are 7,000 pounds unloaded, and the side and bottom wheels are spring loaded to help keep wear down. There are six cars, and five of them can operate at a time. Cars are released from the station and head into a 180-degree left-hand turn in a tunnel. Without stopping, they hit the first set of electromagnets and launch into a vertical climb, where they hit the second set of LSMs. The magnets propel the cars over the 110-foot peak, where they dive straight back down towards the ground. The top speed of 55 mph is reached before flying through an overbanked turn, a zero-g roll, and a series of high speed turns before returning to the station. It's a wicked ride!

30. GATEKEEPER

Known for: Largest wing coaster
Park: Cedar Point
Location: United States
Type: Steel
Opened: 2013
Designer/Manufacturer: Bolliger & Mabillard
Height (ft.): 170
Drop (ft.): 164
Speed (mph): 67
Inversions: 6
Video: http://youtu.be/FxD8SxIsKG8

Cedar Point is known for creating record-breaking coasters, and GateKeeper is no exception. It's the biggest wing coaster built to date, and also has the highest inversion in the world. The first drop slowly turns you upside down, 170 feet in the air, and then sends you into an Immelman loop at 67 mph. After going over a camel back hill and flying through a giant flat spin, riders are faced with the coaster's signature moment: the keyhole fly-throughs. The track forms a zero-g roll over the front entrance to the park while twisting through two 100-foot-tall silver towers. The keyhole openings don't look quite big enough to fit the wide trains through, and passengers feel as if they are going to run right into them!

Coaster enthusiasts often have a specific row or seat that they prefer over the others. On GateKeeper, the consensus is there is no single best seat on the ride. Instead, there are four: front far left, front far right, back far left, and back far right. Sitting on the outside gives the most sensations throughout the very smooth ride. The very front provides the best views of GateKeeper's keyholes and is also the slowest when turning down the first drop. On the other hand, the back whips you down the first drop and is more intense. If you can, ride in all four seats and see for yourself how GateKeeper is different than any other coaster.

29. LAKE PLACID BOBSLED

Known for: Most extreme bobsled-style coaster
Park: Palisades Amusement Park
Location: United States
Type: Wood
Opened: 1937
Closed: 1946
Designer/manufacturer: John Norman Bartlett
Height (ft.): 125
Video: http://youtu.be/ukQNWBKa_BI

The Lake Placid Bobsled was a Flying Turns-style coaster built for Palisades Park, New Jersey, in 1937. It was considered to be the fiercest of the wooden bobsled coasters, but only lasted a mere nine years before it was dismantled in 1946 due to low ridership, rider complaints, and mounting maintenance costs. The Flying Turns-style ride is essentially like a bobsled found in the Winter Olympics, only it runs on wheels and wood instead of blades and ice. Each car sat one or two riders in line and was connected to the other to form a six-car train. The trains were free to roll around the trough, so subsequent rides may not take the exact same path through the course. The Lake Placid Bobsled was known for its out-of-control rides and aggressive nature. Modifications were made over the years to attempt to tame the ride down, but to no avail. Today, the only wooden bobsled coaster in existence is the Flying Turns at Knoebles.

28. STEEL HAWG

Known for: Beyond vertical drop
Park: Indiana Beach
Location: United States
Type: Steel
Opened: 2008
Designer/Manufacturer: S&S Worldwide
Height (ft.): 96
Speed (mph): 41
Inversions: 2
Video: http://www.youtube.com/watch?v=H64idVHWowg

Steel Hawg was the world's steepest roller coaster when it was unleashed at Indiana Beach in 2008. It remains only one of two El Loco model coasters by S&S Worldwide built in the United States. The twisted contraption is simply terrifying to look at it, with its knot of tightly wound track and impossible-looking inversions. Steel Hawg's bright orange track more closely resembles a toy roller coaster assembled out of K'nex than the steel machines built at every other amusement park. After climbing 96 feet, the four-passenger car makes a hairpin turn into a 111-degree first drop. An outside banked turn and two hair-raising inversions filled with out-of-your-seat hang time follow. It's short but oh so sweet!

27. SEQUOIA ADVENTURE

Known for: Upside down track
Park: Gardaland
Location: Italy
Type: Steel
Opened: 2005
Designer/Manufacturer: S&S Worldwide
Height (ft.): 98.4
Inversions: 3
Video: http://www.youtube.com/watch?v=Li5NC8Gdv8o

Sequoia Adventure may be the strangest roller coaster ever built. The majority of the ride is built over the top of itself in a straight line next to the station, with the only two horizontal curves being at the very beginning and end of the ride. The course is mainly composed of three elements known as saxophone inversions, where the cars turn 180 degrees into a flat inverted section of track. Riders spend a considerable amount of time upside down. One way to describe it is like a squirrel scampering along the underside of a tree branch, hence the name of the model: Screaming Squirrel. However, many riders find the extended time spent upside down  to be uncomfortable, which is probably why only three such rides have been built (the others are located in Russia and China). S&S's other compact coaster model, El Loco, and Intamin's ZacSpin coasters have generally filled the Screaming Squirrel's niche.

26. BATMAN (BACKWARDS)

Known for: First inverted roller coaster
Park: Six Flags Great America
Location: United States
Type: Steel
Opened: 1992
Designer/Manufacturer: Bolliger & Mabillard
Height (ft.): 100
Speed (mph): 50
Inversions: 5
Video: http://www.youtube.com/watch?v=iGRbXyZ-c00

Before Alpengeist or Nemesis were even dreamed of, Batman: The Ride became the first inverted roller coaster ever built and was eventually awarded landmark status by the American Coaster Enthusiasts (ACE). The ride was so successful it spawned a dozen clones at amusement parks around the world. After operating the same way for 20 years, Six Flags wanted to do something special and unique. One of their evil geniuses had the brilliant idea to run the ride backwards for a limited time. A special chassis had to be designed and built in order for it to work. What was already an intense experience was instantly magnified. Just going up the lift backwards, not being able to see the top and having to stare at the ground, increased the scariness factor. Coaster enthusiasts affectionately labeled this version of the ride "Namtab" (Batman spelled backwards).

25. FLIGHT OF FEAR

Known for: First LIM launch coaster
Park: Kings Island
Location: United States
Type: Steel
Opened: 1996
Designer/Manufacturer: Premier Rides
Height (ft.): 74.2
Inversions: 4
Video: http://youtu.be/UnBTtDY5BBk

In 1996, The Outer Limits: Flight of Fear at Kings Island became the first roller coaster to use electromagnetic propulsion instead of the traditional chain lift (the Outer Limits portion of the name was dropped before the start of the 2001 season, when the licensing agreement expired). The restraints were also changed in 2001, from over-the-shoulder harnesses to individual lap bars. Flight of Fear was manufactured by Premier, and its highest point is 74 feet tall. All 2,705 feet of track are enclosed in a large warehouse-type building. Earthlings enter the attraction through a large alien spaceship. The electromagnetic launch takes three megawatts of power to accelerate the trains from zero to 60 mph in less than four seconds. Abductees are flown threw four inversions, but it seems like many more than that when you're flying around in the darkness.

How does it work? Linear induction motors use multiple sets of high-powered electromagnets secured to the track, and a gap is left in between each set. Alternating current (AC) is applied to the magnets to create a magnetic field. A metal fin attached to the bottom of the train passes through the gap in the magnets while the magnetic field creates a wave for the fin to ride and propels the train forward down the track. Flight of Fear paved the way for many taller and faster launched coasters.

24. EL TORO

Known for: Currently world's fastest wooden roller coaster
Park: Six Flags Great Adventure
Location: United States
Type: Wood
Opened: 2006
Designer/Manufacturer: Intamin AG
Height (ft.): 181
Drop (ft.): 176
Speed (mph): 70
Video: http://www.youtube.com/watch?v=YnE4PdvLG3Q

El Toro, or "The Bull" in Spanish, is a wooden roller coaster at Six Flags Great Adventure that opened to the public on June 11, 2006. It was designed by Intamin of Switzerland and had the steepest drop of any wooden roller coaster in the world at 76 degrees (the record was broken by T Express in 2008 by one degree). El Toro is revered for the extreme negative g-forces (airtime) riders experience over the large parabolic-shaped hills.

Besides being one of the tallest and fastest wooden coasters, it may also be the most technologically advanced. It was the first wooden roller coaster to use a cable lift hill instead of the traditional chain lift. El Toro is the only coaster in the United States to use industrially prefabricated wooden track segments, which were shipped to the construction site and mounted directly to the support structures, similar to a modern steel coaster. The rails can be milled to a precise form with a very tight tolerance in a machine shop, not only improving the ride experience but also reducing construction time and increasing service life. The pieces of track are then fixed to each bent, creating a more rigid system (as opposed to the traditional wooden coaster track that floats more freely on the structure). In fact, El Toro is so smooth that enthusiasts argue it should no longer be considered a wood coaster, and should be classified as something entirely different.

23. THE SMILER

Known for: World recorder holder for most inversions
Park: Alton Towers
Location: United States
Type: Steel
Opened: 2013
Designer/Manufacturer: Gerstlauer Amusement Rides GmbH
Height (ft.): 72
Drop (ft.): 98.4
Speed (mph): 52.8
Inversions: 14
Video: http://www.youtube.com/watch?v=qqN9PDS3hOc

It's time to get corrected. Alton Towers' latest "Secret Weapon" (the code name for their roller coasters still in development), The Smiler is their longest coaster to date, with 3,838 feet of seriously convoluted track. You'll be whipped upside down 14 times, more than any other coaster on the planet. Two inverted drops, a batwing, a cobra roll—pretty much any type of inversion element you can think of is included in this one ride.

All has not been smooth sailing at the Towers since the completion of The Smiler, as the world record-breaking roller coaster has faced multiple mechanical and technical issues. Incidents have ranged from the train becoming stuck on the first lift hill and passengers being trapped in their seats for an hour before being evacuated from the ride to a major scare in July of 2013, when 48 people were evacuated from the ride after a piece of debris fell from a section of track. Eyewitnesses described the debris as a bolt that dropped from the coaster, which partially disengaged two sections of track, forcing the ride to close for inspection. The Smiler reopened four days later.

22. G-FORCE

Known for: Inverted lift hill
Park: Drayton Manor
Location: United Kingdom
Type: Steel
Opened: 2005
Designer/Manufacturer: Maurer Söhne
Height (ft.): 82
Speed (mph): 43.5
Inversions: 3
Video: http://www.youtube.com/watch?v=sDibFwuWHPE

G-Force was only the second Maurer Söhne X-Car coaster to be built in the world (the first being the prototype Sky Wheel at Skyline Park in Germany). Drayton Manor's new, state-of-the-art roller coaster features wide-open X-Car trains, lap bars (remember that), and a capacity of 1,000 people an hour. The most terrifying feature of G-Force is the humpty-bump lift hill where terrified riders are pulled up the first half of a vertical loop until they are completely inverted. And, yes, inverted means upside down. You'll be begging for mercy and

the ride has barely begun. After being released from the weird lift the inverted vehicles swoop down, finish the loop, reach a speed of 40 mph, and complete the rest of the coaster's twisted circuit, including a unique double inversion known as a bent Cuban eight. It's another small, compact layout but it throws quite the punch!

21. DÉJÀ VU

Known for: Vertical forwards and backwards drops
Park: Six Flags Great America
Location: United States
Type: Steel
Opened: 2001
Closed: 2007
Designer/Manufacturer: Vekoma
Height (ft.): 191.6
Drop (ft.): 177
Speed (mph): 65.6
Inversions: 3
Video: http://www.youtube.com/watch?v=TXZ79NhMXEs

In 2001, Six Flags took a huge gamble and built three of Vekoma's new "Giant Inverted Boomerang" roller coaster prototypes at different theme parks throughout the chain—one each at Magic Mountain, Great America, and Over Georgia. The identical rides featured inverted cars, a 102-foot-tall loop, and a 110-foot-tall cobra roll. The trains are pulled up a vertical tower before being released to travel along the 1,200-foot-long track twice, once forward and once backward. Initially, the giant inverted boomerangs were plagued with problems. In 2008, Déjà Vu was removed from Six Flags Great America and relocated to Silverwood Theme Park in Idaho, where it is now known as Aftershock.

20. ABISMO

Known for: Skyloop inversion
Park: Parque de Atracciones de Madrid
Location: Spain
Type: Steel
Opened: 2006
Designer/Manufacturer: Maurer Söhne
Height (ft.): 151.6
Speed (mph): 65.2
Inversions: 2
Video: http://www.youtube.com/watch?v=c9obwQdRt44

Maurer Söhne is known for their crazy-looking SkyLoop roller coaster model, and the most terrifying of the bunch is Abismo at Parque de Atracciones de Madrid in Spain. While the popular model installed at several parks is the XT 150, Abismo is an XT 450, and is the only extended SkyLoop in the world. The trains are made up of two X-Cars that seat six passengers each. The trains depart from the station and immediately begin the climb up the head-pinned-against-the-seatback vertical lift. But rather than cresting out and dropping down like Hollywood Rip Ride Rockit, Abismo goes the other route and slowly flips upside down. Riders hang inverted 150 feet in the air and hope they secured their cell phones. The train negotiates a heartline roll and drops back to Earth, reaching 65 mph in the process. Some overbanked turns and airtime-filled camel back hills round out the 1,345-foot-long coaster before returning to the station.

19. DODONPA

Known for: Fastest accelerating coaster
Park: Fuji-Q Highland
Location: Japan
Type: Steel
Opened: 2001
Designer/Manufacturer: S&S Worldwide
Height (ft.): 170.6
Drop (ft.): 50
Speed (mph): 106.9
Video: http://www.youtube.com/watch?v=ZqPykRYD5Bw

Dodonpa, located at Fuji-Q Highland, was the fastest roller coaster in the world when it opened in 2001, and just the second coaster ever to utilize the power of compressed air to launch its trains. Today, it's no longer the fastest overall, but it still holds the record for fastest acceleration—a mind-blowing 106.9 mph in 1.8 seconds! The launch system is similar to the hydraulic launch found on Intamin's accelerator coasters in that a cable pulls a catch car that connects underneath the train. If the launch isn't enough to terrify you, then maybe the ninety-degree vertical climb up the 170-foot-tall tower and subsequent fall straight back down will. Interestingly, the cars use rubber tires instead of the typical steel or polyurethane found on most coasters. And in case you were wondering, the name "Dodonpa" comes from the notes used by taiko drummers.

18. X-FLIGHT

Known for: Steel flying roller coaster
Park: Geauga Lake
Location: United States
Type: Steel
Opened: 2001
Closed: 2006
Designer/Manufacturer: Vekoma
Height (ft.): 115
Drop (ft.): 80
Speed (mph): 50
Inversions: 5
Video: http://www.youtube.com/watch?v=K-OFWEfDSdE

X-Flight was one of only two 1018M Flying Dutchman coasters manufactured by Vekoma. This flying coaster uses a unique double station to increase capacity due to the slow boarding process. Riders board the train sitting up first, then, once riders have been loaded and strapped into the vests and lap bars, the train is lowered into the lying position. Exiting the station, the train heads up a 115-foot lift hill with the riders lying on their back and unable to see where they're going. Once the train leaves the lift, it turns into the first lie-to-fly element, dropping face first at 50 mph into a horseshoe overbanked turn. Riders are then flipped from fly-to-lie and into the 66-foot-tall vertical loop. Going from lie-to-fly again, the coaster then takes a turn into the double in-line twist, then into the helix, where it finishes with another fly-to-lie into the brake run. X-Flight was relocated from Geauga Lake to Kings Island in 2007.

17. THIRTEEN

Known for: First freefall dropping track element
Park: Alton Towers
Location: United Kingdom
Type: Steel
Opened: 2010
Designer/manufacturer: Intamin AG
Height (ft.): 60
Drop (ft.): 56
Speed (mph): 41
Video: http://www.youtube.com/watch?v=OgHMgJPtg4E

The third coaster from Alton Towers to make this list is the one they call "the scariest ride in the UK." The park promised that Thirteen, built on the site of the old Corkscrew rollercoaster (which was removed), would combine physical and psychological fear elements that would be so terrifying it would breed a new type of thrill ride—the "psychoaster." The storyline is that visitors are invited to take a petrifying ride on Thirteen, venturing into the seemingly living and breathing Dark Forest. There they face an unknown horror that has been unleashed from an ancient crypt.

After a thrilling ride through the forest, the trains enter the ancient crypt. A door closes behind the trains, pitching the room into complete darkness. Suddenly, the track drops out from underneath and the train drops. Thirteen is the world's first vertical freefall drop roller coaster, on which the track and train freefall approximately fifteen feet in total darkness. Once at the bottom there's no time to catch your breath, as the train speeds backwards into a helix and emerges back outside. Finally, the out-of-control train stops and proceeds forward into the loading station.

16. MILLENNIUM FORCE

Known for: First full circuit coaster to break 300 feet
Park: Cedar Point
Location: United States
Type: Steel
Opened: 2000
Designer/Manufacturer: Intamin AG
Height (ft.): 310
Drop (ft.): 300
Speed (mph): 93
Video: http://www.youtube.com/watch?v=jbXPhOFRxTc

The coaster world was taken by storm with the stunning announcement of Millennium Force at Cedar Point. The biggest investment in the park's storied history would be the first roller coaster with a complete circuit to break the 300-foot mark (though its record would be broken a few months later by Steel Dragon 2000). The ride's stats were ridiculous and had coaster enthusiasts all over the world salivating: 310 feet tall, 80-degree drop, 93 mph, and over 6,000 feet of track. The last hill on Millennium Force is taller than a large majority of other coasters. A ride this size was unheard of at the time.

Millennium Force would pave the way for a new era in coasters, and employed new technology. It was the first coaster to use a cable lift to quickly pull the nine-car train up its mammoth 310-foot-tall lift hill in 22 seconds. A relatively new variation on the chain lift, the cable system allows for a faster and steeper lift hill, which is often quiet because the anti-rollback devices are electromagnetically disengaged by the passing train and automatically close after it passes. The cable is connected to a catch car that rides on its own guide in the middle of the track. The catch car attaches underneath the vehicle so that the train is pulled to the top of the lift hill as the cable is wound up on a giant drum.

Millennium Force graces the top of many coaster enthusiasts' best ride lists, and is often considered the best roller coaster in the world. It paved the way for larger rides, including Top Thrill Dragster, which came just three years later.

15. FORMULA ROSA

Known for: World's fastest roller coaster
Park: Ferrari World
Location: UAE
Type: Steel
Opened: 2010
Designer: Intamin
Height (ft.): 174
Drop (ft.): 169
Speed (mph): 150

Formula Rossa is a hydraulic launched roller coaster located at Ferrari World in Abu Dhabi, United Arab Emirates. Manufactured by Intamin, this is the world's fastest roller coaster, with a top speed of 240 km/h (150 mph). The coaster train accelerates to its top speed in approximately 4.9 seconds using a hydraulic launch system that generates a release velocity similar to that of aircraft carrier steam catapults. High speeds combined with the risk of an impact with airborne particulates (like sand or insects) results in riders being required to wear protective glasses similar to those used while skydiving. The layout is mostly comprised of a large figure eight with low-to-the-ground turns and a series of bunny hops back towards the station. While many launched coasters shoot right into a large, oftentimes vertical hill, Formula Rossa launches into a more drawn-out hill.

14. VOYAGE

Known for: 24.2 seconds of airtime
Park: Holiday World
Location: United States
Type: Wood
Opened: 2006
Designer/Manufacturer: The Gravity Group, LLC
Height (ft.): 163
Drop (ft.): 154
Speed (mph): 67.4
Video: http://www.youtube.com/watch?v=JtUj-sEq3JE

Santa Claus, Indiana, may not be where you would expect to find one of the most terrifying roller coasters in the world, but it's where the Voyage calls home. Located in the Thanksgiving themed region of Holiday World, the Voyage was ranked as the best wooden roller coaster by the Golden Ticket Awards from 2007 through 2011. This 1.2-mile coaster offers more "airtime" than any other wooden coaster in the world, an amazing 24 seconds! The highlight of the journey is a triple-down in a tunnel. This is a series of three drops in a row, with each drop getting progressively larger and steeper. There's also a station fly-through, more tunnels, and a spaghetti bowl turnaround deep in the middle of the woods. The ride is a trial of sheer intensity and can feel like a workout. A common complaint about the mega-coasters of the modern era is that they're too short. For many pilgrims, the Voyage may be the first ride that is actually too long.

13. STEEL DRAGON 2000

Known for: World's tallest non-launched coaster
Park: Nagashima Spa Land
Location: Japan
Type: Steel
Opened: 2000
Designer/Manufacturer: Steve Okamoto
Height (ft.): 318.3
Drop (ft.): 306.8
Speed (mph): 95
Video: http://www.youtube.com/watch?v=JnsOhtNSYqw

Steel Dragon 20000 opened a few months after Cedar Point's Millennium Force and stole the world's tallest coaster title. To this day it reigns as the world's tallest non-launched roller coaster. Impressively, Steel Dragon 2000 is the only coaster in the world to break the 8,000-foot length threshold. Four minutes may not seem like much, but it can be a loooooong time on a coaster—particularly one that rises a staggering 318 feet and reaches a mind-numbing speed of 95 mph. For only the second time in the company's history, B&M provided trains for a coaster they didn't build. The coaster did not operate from 2003 to 2006 due to a sheered axle that caused one of the original train's cars to lose a wheel. The ride reopened sporting two new, sleek B&M trains seating 28 riders sitting two abreast. Earthquake protection was a huge concern, so the structure uses far more steel then similar rides, which is why the cost ballooned to over $50 million dollars. (In comparison, Millennium Force's cost was just a cool $25 million).

12. GRIFFON

Known for: Vertical drop with pause at top
Park: Busch Gardens Williamsburg
Location: United States
Type: Steel
Opened: 2007
Designer/Manufacturer: Bolliger & Mabillard
Height (ft.): 205
Speed (mph): 71
Inversions: 2
Similar: Sheikra at Busch Gardens Tampa and Diving Coaster at Happy Valley
Video: http://youtu.be/tdl8wnQOkjM

Griffon materialized at Busch Gardens Williamsburg in May 18, 2007, replacing the Le Mans Raceway antique car ride in the New France section of the park. It was the first dive coaster with floorless trains, and the only coaster of its kind to feature multiple inversions. A Bolliger and Mabillard creation, Griffon stands 205 feet high, just 5 feet shy of the first drop on Apollo's Chariot, the park's other hyper coaster. This mythical creature features not one but two 90-degree vertical drops, two Immelman loops, and a "splash down" near the ride's finale. Riders sit 10 across in three "stadium-style" rows, making it one of the widest coaster trains ever built. The middle four riders in each row are over the track, while the three riders on the left and right side of each row are suspended in mid-air. The most heart pounding moment is the dreaded pause before the big drop. The cars perch on the edge of the massive 200-foot, ninety-degree vertical drop for several seconds, letting the riders ponder their fate before finally being released and hitting the max speed of 71 mph. That'll wake you up in the morning.

11. FLIP-FLAP RAILWAY

Known for: First looping coaster in North America
Park: Paul Boyton's Sea Lion Park
Location: United States
Type: Wood
Opened: 1895
Closed: 1902
Designer/manufacturer: Lina Beecher
Inversions: 1

The Flip-Flap Railway was one of the first looping roller coasters in the world. The "highlight" of the ride (if you want to call it that) was a 25-foot circular loop. To make it all the way around without being pulled off by gravity at the top, the coaster's cars hit the circle hard and fast, shoving riders' heads into their chests as they changed direction with a sudden snap, resulting in whiplash and sore necks. It's been said that the Flip-Flap produced as many as 12 Gs, enough to knock some passengers unconscious. Safety standards at the time weren't what they are today.

Flip-Flap Railway closed in 1902 due to its low popularity. There weren't very many repeat customers, as those who survived the ordeal considered it to be more of a torture device than a thrill ride. Another contributing factor was the ride's low capacity, seating only two passengers in a single car, meaning profits were low. But the coaster probably wouldn't have lasted much longer anyways because Sea Lion Park would close the following year and be replaced by Luna Park in 1903.

As for looping roller coasters, well, the inversion wasn't perfected until the 1970s, when the Corkscrew at Knott's Berry Farm became the first modern (and successful) looping roller coaster. Circular loops were done away with and replaced by elliptical shaped loops that kept the forces on the riders low and tolerable throughout the duration of the inversion.

10. TATSU

Known for: Giant pretzel loop inversion
Park: Six Flags Magic Mountain
Location: United States
Type: Steel
Opened: 2006
Designer/Manufacturer: Bolliger & Mabillard
Height (ft.): 170
Drop (ft.): 111
Speed (mph): 62
Inversions: 4
Video: http://www.youtube.com/watch?v=p2VXzbtf9uA

    The world's tallest, fastest, and longest flying coaster debuted at Six Flags Magic Mountain in 2006. Thanks to its hilly terrain, Tatsu glides more than 100 feet above terra firma at times, delivering on its slogan to "Fly at the speed of fear." This dragon—or winged beast, as it is referred to in Japanese mythology—is the pinnacle of the flying coaster model. The 111-foot swooping first drop, zero-gravity roll, and horseshoe turn are fun, but are merely a warm-up for what comes next. Tatsu features the world's largest pretzel loop, and it just may be the most intense inversion on the planet. As opposed to a typical vertical loop, the trains start at the highest point and dive headfirst toward the ground, putting riders onto their backs before heading towards the sky and completing the loop. Impressively, the base of Tatsu's pretzel loop is a full 263 feet below the crest of the lift hill, and is where it reaches its top speed of 62 mph. Taking a flight on Tatsu may be the closest you'll ever come to the experience of flying like a dragon.

9. INTIMIDATOR 305

Known for: Innovative support structure
Park: Kings Dominion
Location: United States
Type: Steel
Opened: 2010
Designer/Manufacturer: Intamin AG
Height (ft.): 305
Drop (ft.): 300
Speed (mph): 90
Video: http://youtu.be/oOR8brK9Dqg

Thrill seekers wanting to get their hearts racing need only to travel to Doswell, Virginia, to challenge the Intimidator 305, one of only three giga coasters in North America. At 305 feet (the 305 part of its name), it's higher than the observation platform of Kings Dominion's Eiffel Tower replica. Themed to NASCAR legend Dale Earnhardt, not only was it voted best new coaster when it debuted in 2010, but it cracked the top 10 coasters in the world list for the Golden Ticket Awards by *Amusement Park Today*. The cable-driven lift hill and 85-degree first drop is supported by a unique arch-style arrangement. It's a very minimalistic support system compared to Millennium Force's steel intensive truss system that was built by Intamin just 10 years earlier.

While Kings Dominion wanted an extreme roller coaster, they ended up getting more than they bargained for. Within a few weeks of operation the park received complaints from guests about the ride being too intense. A majority of the riders found it to be more nauseous than fun, and complained about the high g-forces experienced in the first turn following the giant first drop. Additionally, the maintenance department had to replace wheels much more frequently than any other coaster in the park. The extreme g-forces and heavy trains resulted in significant wheel usage, especially in hot weather conditions. Wheels were lasting only several days during the summer, with multiple modes of failure. As a short-term fix, the park added trim brakes to the first drop to slow it down — a coaster enthusiast's worst nightmare! In the offseason after its first season, the entire first turn and climb were re-profiled — the entire section of track was replaced, a very costly endeavor. The restraints on the vehicles were also changed to a softer material to prevent head banging during the high-speed side-to-side maneuvers.

8. OUTLAW RUN

Known for: Most inversions on a wood coaster
Park: Silver Dollar City
Location: United States
Type: Wood
Opened: 2013
Designer/Manufacturer: Rocky Mountain Construction
Height (ft.): 107
Drop (ft.): 162
Speed (mph): 68
Inversions: 3
Video: http://youtu.be/1n0hTR0l6KU

Relative newcomers on the coaster design scene, Rocky Mountain Construction have developed a new wooden coaster technology. "Topper track" replaces the top two pieces of a wood coaster's stack with steel and allows wooden coasters to do things they've never done before (and maybe were never meant to do). One of these new hybrid wooden coasters opened in 2013 at Silver Dollar City. Outlaw Run was the first wooden roller coaster with multiple inversions and the first looping wooden coaster since Son of Beast's loop was removed in 2006. The first drop is insane: 163 feet at 81 degrees. The train plunges toward the earth at 68 mph towards three elements that have never been seen on a wooden coaster before—a 153-degree inverting overbanked turn, a double barrel roll, and a wave turn that provides lateral airtime.

7. INSANE

Known for: Unpredictable ride experience
Park: Grona Lund
Location: Sweden
Type: Steel
Opened: 2009
Designer/Manufacturer: Intamin AG
Height (ft.): 116.5
Speed (mph): 37.3
Inversions: Variable
Similar: Green Lantern at Six Flags Magic Mountain
Video: http://youtu.be/uTXdHs61hYI

If you enjoy backflips and somersaults, this is the ride for you (though you'll have to travel to Sweden to ride it)! As its name suggests, Insane is a crazy ride with multiple changes in direction and wild, unpredictable spinning. It's the tallest Intamin Zac Spin or "ball coaster" in the world, where the seats are cantilevered to either side of the vehicle and are free to rotate 360 degrees head-over-heels (or vice versa). The ride is stacked on top of itself in a vertical manner—there are no horizontal curves to speak of, but you won't be missing them on this monster. If you have a weak stomach, you better pray the sadistic ride ops don't load the cars with uneven weight distribution. The spinning motion is produced by the vehicles' momentum, and thus no two rides are exactly the same. It's probably a good idea not to eat anything immediately before going for a spin on Insane.

6. SUPERMAN: THE ESCAPE

Known for: First coaster to break 100mph
Park: Six Flags Magic Mountain
Location: United States
Type: Steel
Opened: 1997
Designer/Manufacturer: Intamin AG
Height (ft.): 415
Drop (ft.): 328.1
Speed (mph): 100
Video: http://www.youtube.com/watch?v=JAYjWKAvysc
Similar: Tower of Terror II at Dreamworld

A roller coaster reaching speeds of 100 mph? It was unthinkable. That is, until Superman: The Escape opened in 1997. With the use of linear synchronous motors (LSMs) the car is accelerated from zero to 100 mph in seven heart-pounding seconds. LSMs use the basic magnetism theories of attraction and repulsion. Strong, permanent, rare-earth (those that come out of the ground magnetized) magnets are attached to the train. As with LIMs, electro-magnets are secured to the track. When the train approaches one of the track-magnets, the track-magnet is set to attract the magnets on the train, pulling the train forward. After the train passes over the track-magnet, the track-magnet is reversed to repel the train magnet, pushing the train down the track. Multiple sets of electro-magnets on the track must be fired in sequence, switching polarity very quickly by the use of computers and electricity, in order to propel the train to top speed. Riders experience several blissful seconds of airtime before falling back to Earth and returning down the same track they were launched from (the track is not a complete circuit and looks like a giant L).

For the 2011 season, Superman: The Escape was

transformed into Superman: Escape from Krypton. The most significant change was turning the vehicles around to face backwards so passengers were initially launched backwards rather than forwards, and looked towards the ground rather than the sky on the vertical track.

5. SON OF BEAST

Known for: First looping modern wooden coaster
Park: Kings Island
Location: United States
Type: Wood
Opened: 2000
Closed: 2009
Height (ft.): 218
Drop (ft.): 214
Speed (mph): 78.4
Inversions: 1
Video: http://www.youtube.com/watch?v=e7wRvjbWnmQ

Anytime a Hollywood movie is successful, a sequel is made. The same can now be said of roller coasters. Based on the success and popularity of The Beast, Kings Island decided to make a "sequel" ride, dubbed Son of Beast. The son would outdo the father in many ways. It was the tallest and fastest wooden roller coaster ever built, and the first wooden hyper coaster. Son of Beast smashed nearly every wooden coaster record, except that it was designed as the second longest wooden roller coaster so that The Beast could retain the record. The most incredible and terrifying feature was the 118-foot-tall vertical loop. Although the supports for the loop were formed from steel, Son of Beast was still the first modern looping wooden coaster in the world. In fact, Son of Beast also once held the record for longest roller coaster with a loop (a record now held by California Screamin' at Disney California Adventure).

After numerous problems and an accident, the vertical loop was removed at the end of the 2006 season for maintenance reasons. After another incident, Son of Beast was closed in 2009 and left standing but not operating (SBNO) for many years (and thirty something million dollars down the drain). Ironically, the ride was located in the Action Zone section of the park, but was out of action for many years. Finally, in July 2012, it was announced that the ride would be dismantled and removed from the park later that year.

All that remains of Son of Beast today is the station.

4. KINGDA KA

Known for: World's tallest roller coaster
Park: Six Flags Great Adventure
Location: United States
Type: Steel
Opened: 2005
Designer/Manufacturer: Intamin AG
Height (ft.): 456
Drop (ft.): 418
Speed (mph): 128
Video:
http://youtu.be/7om9O0eXIpg
Similar: Top Thrill Dragster at Cedar Point

    Kingda Ka at Six Flags Great Adventure in Jackson, New Jersey, is the world's tallest free-standing roller coaster. This king of coasters is launched by a hydraulic motor to 128 mph (206 km/h) in 3.5 seconds, making it the second faster coaster in the world. At the end of the launch track, the train climbs the main top hat tower, reaching a record-breaking height of 456 feet (139 m) before spiraling straight down. The train speeds into a second hill of 129 feet before smoothly slowing to a stop via magnetic brakes. The entire ride covers the 3,118-foot-long (950 m) track in less than a minute, but it's one that will stick with you forever.

    Here's how it works: Hydraulic launch systems utilize a catch car (called a sled) connected to a cable, which latches onto a mechanism attached to the underside of the coaster train. The catch car moves in its own track or "groove" in the center of the launch track. The hydraulic motor is located at one end of the launch track, and the waiting train at the other. Think of it like a giant fishing pole that reels a train in super fast before being released.

3. GRAVITY MAX

Known for: World's only tilt coaster
Park: Lihpao Land
Location: Taiwan
Type: Steel
Opened: 2002
Designer/Manufacturer: Vekoma
Height (ft.): 114
Speed (mph): 56
Inversions: 1
Video: http://www.youtube.com/watch?v=aA4_BjmHzAM

     Gravity Max in Taiwan's Discovery World theme park is the world's only "tilt coaster." The coaster begins innocently enough, ascending a typical chain lift hill. But, upon cresting the apex, riders notice the track suddenly ends! The rails stop and there is nothing but blue sky. The train keeps moving until it reaches the end of the track, where it thankfully stops. What happens next will blow your mind—the entire section of track the vehicle is now sitting on rotates 90 degrees. The riders are now staring straight down and praying, "I hope the rails are lined up!" The movable segment is locked into the next section of track and, without warning, the train is released. After the vertical drop into a tunnel, riders are subjected to a forceful turn, a vertical loop, and a gut-wrenching helix before returning flummoxed to the station. Those twisted Dutch thrill ride designers at Vekoma had the audacity to build this crazy contraption—the only one like it in the world today, and a truly terrifying coaster.

2. X2

Known for: World's first 4th dimension coaster
Park: Six Flags Magic Mountain
Location: United States
Type: Steel
Opened: 2002
Designer/Manufacturer: Arrow Dynamics / S&S Power
Height (ft.): 175
Drop (ft.): 215
Speed (mph): 76
Inversions: 2
Video: http://youtu.be/8WTD0Hc9anw
Similar: Dinoconda at China Dinosaurs Park and Eejanaika at Fuji-Q Highland

On its own, a coaster with a 215-foot near vertical drop would be terrifying enough to make this list. But that's not all X2 has to offer — the seats can rotate forward or backward 360 degrees in a controlled spin. It's like a spin-and-puke carnival ride and a hyper coaster had a lovechild together. The demented designers at Arrow drew up this wicked machine, which was later perfected by S&S Power. X2 was the first 4th dimension wing coaster where the controlled spinning or rotation of the seats is in a direction that is independent of the track — hence the "fourth dimension" designation. There are two sets of rails — one supports the weight of the vehicles while the other is what makes the seats rotate. The vertical distance or displacement between the two sets of rails controls the rotation of the passengers by transforming linear motion into rotational motion, accomplished via a rack and pinion gear.

Riders depart the station facing backwards, so the long climb up the hill is quite agonizing. Let's just get this over with! Before long, the top of the hill is reached. Then, after a small dip, the seats rotate forward, bringing you around to face the ground 200 feet below you. You drop face first, straight down, before rotating onto your back midway through the drop. After the first drop, the train enters an inside raven loop. As it exits the loop, the seats rotate, executing a "lie-to-fly" maneuver, transitioning the riders from lying on their backs above the track facing backwards to a flying position hanging under the track facing forward. Shortly after exiting the first vertical turn and while still in the flying position, the seats do a 360-degree rotation backwards, completing a full backflip. Meanwhile, the train performs a unique half-twist/forward flip. This transitions the train back on top of the track and the riders onto their backs, looking backward again. This is also referred to as a "fly-to-lie" maneuver. As soon as you get your bearings, giant flame throwers spit fire overhead, leaving you in awe.

No matter how many coaster notches you have on your belt, you've never experienced anything quite like X2—the most terrifying roller coaster you can ride today.

1. CRYSTAL BEACH CYCLONE

Known for: Nurse in the station
Park: Crystal Beach
Location: Canada
Type: Wood
Opened: 1926
Closed: 1946
Designer/Manufacturer: Harry G. Traver
Height (ft.): 96
Drop (ft.): 90
Speed (mph): 60
Video: http://www.youtube.com/watch?v=9hMveMFnigM

The Crystal Beach Cyclone is considered to be the most extreme roller coaster ever built. The mother of all roller coasters was spawned in 1927 at Crystal Beach Amusement Park in Ontario, Canada. For over 20 years this demonic creation terrorized over five million victims, dragging them through its demented dives, twisted turns, and wickedly warped trackage. While its 96-foot-tall lift hill may be relatively small by today's standards, the Cyclone made up for lack of height with rapid fire transitions and perverted elements, such as 80-degree banked turns, a high speed figure-eight, jazz-track (trick track), and tiny one-foot bunny hops. Although this terrifying trip lasted only around 40 seconds after cresting the lift, there was almost no straight track to be found. The unrelenting pace made the ride so severe it was probably more than most riders could handle.

In fact, what made the Cyclone even more notorious was the employment of a full-time nurse in the station to treat passengers coming off the ride. Common ailments were aches, pains, stiff necks, and fainting, either due to fear or being knocked unconscious by the ride's forces. A few accounts from actual survivors of the Cyclone claim the station constantly reeked of vomit. How much of this is true we'll never know, but it certainly adds to the mystique of the ride.

On September 2nd, 1946, the Crystal Beach Cyclone closed forever. About two weeks later, the dismantling of the Cyclone started. Some of the wood and steel was used to create the Crystal Beach Comet in 1948. Not only stress on the passengers, but to the structure itself led to its eventual demise.

Despite the coaster's intensity, only one rider was killed when he was thrown from the train after his lap bar failed. Because of today's strict safety standards, we will probably never see another ride like it.

The twisted track of the Crystal Beach Cyclone

Terrifying Coaster Statistics

Where are the most terrifying rides found? Who designs them? Which park builds the craziest rides? Find the answers in the terrifying coaster statistics summary below:

Type
Steel: 40
Wood: 10

Amusement Park
Kings Island: 4
Six Flags Magic Mountain: 4
Cedar Point: 3

Designer
Bolliger & Mabillard: 9
Intamin AG: 8
Vekoma: 3
Premier Rides: 3

Country
United States: 34
United Kingdom: 4
Japan: 2
Canada: 2

Status
Currently operating: 42
Defunct: 8

Continent
North America: 36
Europe: 7
Asia: 5
Africa: 1
Australia: 1

Features
Number that go upside down: 29 (58%)
Number that go backwards: 8 (16%)
Number that feature a vertical lift or drop: 16 (32%)

The Next Generation of Terror

Roller coaster designers are constantly innovating and pushing the limits as fans crave wilder and crazier rides. Since the first edition of this book was published, Kings Island opened Banshee, the world's longest inverted coaster, and Six Flags Great America erected the world's steepest and fastest wood coaster. What does the future hold? A peek over the horizon shows some innovative upcoming coasters will come online soon:

Orlando's Skyscraper will be the world's tallest roller coaster. This "poler coaster" will smash Kingda Ka's height record and will be the first over 500 feet tall. Cannibal at Lagoon Park will use an elevator lift followed by the world's steepest drop. ZDT's Switchback is a shuttle coaster made out of wood! This Gravity Group woodie will also be the first shuttle coaster with a full chain lift and first drop experience. And a Dynamic Attractions multi-direction coaster could be built at Ferrari World which will feature movable track segments.

Maybe the most interesting upcoming roller coaster is Batman: The Ride, expected to open at Six Flags Fiesta Texas in summer of 2015 as the first 4D free fly coaster by S&S Sansei. The new coaster has been compared to the very similar looking Insane at Grona Lund, a Zac Spin coaster by Intamin. While a rather unique ride experience, the reviews for Insane have mostly ranged from average to not favorable with many riders complaining about the lack of comfort.

Because the two rides look similar, many coaster enthusiasts are already worried about the ride experience on Batman. But if we look closer we'll see there are a few key differences in Batman's favor. Here are three potential improvements:

Let's start with the track. Batman is using Rocky Mountain Construction's Iron Horse track (though it is a larger variation than found on the wooden makeovers). It's easier to cut and weld flat pieces of steel than bending a round tube, as Rocky Mountain explains in their track patent:

"WHEN STEEL ROD OR STEEL PIPE IS HEATED AND BENT INTO COMPLEX DESIGNS, THE ROD OR PIPE DOES NOT NECESSARILY BEND AS DESIRED. METAL WILL TYPICALLY SEEK TO BEND AT ITS WEAKEST POINT OR WHERE THE MOST FORCE IS APPLIED OVER A SPAN. AS SUCH, THE END RESULT OF A FABRICATED STEEL STRUCTURE MAY NOT EXACTLY MATCH THE DESIRED DESIGN, WHICH EITHER RESULTS IN REPEATED ATTEMPTS OF FABRICATION OR SETTLING FOR A LESS THAN OPTIMAL RESULT."
http://www.google.com/patents/US8590455

So the Iron Horse track will be much more precise than a traditional steel coaster – something that takes on even more importance when you're creating wide trains with seats sticking out away from the center of gravity. I expect Batman to be much smoother as this type of track makes it easier to maintain plane resulting in no extra flapping or bouncing and less vibration than the zac spins or previous 4D coasters.

Have you ever watched a gymnast while she's doing a front flip? Where is the center of rotation at? The gymnast rotates somewhere around their midsection. Batman will use a similar center of rotation. Compare that to a Zac Spin car where riders sit back to back and the axis of rotation is somewhere behind you. The positioning of the axis of rotation near rider's midsections should result in more natural feeling flips.

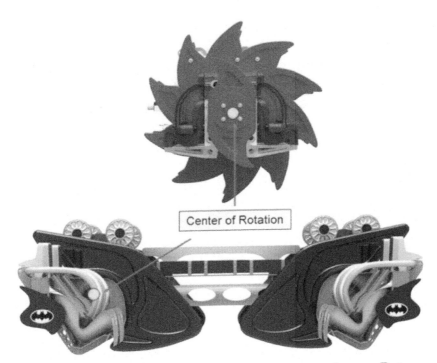

Center of Rotation

Additionally, the way the spinning works on Batman is pretty much controlled chaos. The seat rotation design is pretty similar to the 4D trains Arrow patented and then S&S acquired when they took over the assets, just that they don't have the rack and pinion mechanism that controls the rotation. The seats are free to spin but they also have a magnet and fin system that helps control the flipping. There are actually two sets of magnets: the first prevents the spinning from becoming too fast or too much while the second can be used to help induce spinning to flip the seats at the desired locations.

One of the issues with the free spinning Zac Spins is the spinning is totally dependent on weight distribution, and that can sometimes lead to less favorable rides. The magnets on Batman prevent this problem from happening. The coaster designers have also stated that if you get two passengers moving their limbs in tandem at the right moments, the riders can actually affect the spin of the seats –

how cool is that? We won't know for sure until the ride actually opens, but for these three reasons Batman: The Ride could be the best utilization of spinning seats on a coaster ever built and it's just another reason why the future is looking very bright for those who like to get their pants scared off.

White Knuckle Rides

Roller coasters exist to provide us with a break from everyday life. They create an exhilarating—and often addicting—distraction from the experiences our senses are used to. The feeling of being out of control without any real danger is not easy to come by. By nature, humans are programmed to go looking for danger. Skydiving, mountaineering, and racing are just a few of the many sports man indulges in just for the thrill of it. Not everyone is such a daredevil, however, so thrill rides give people the ability to enjoy these dangers without the danger element. Pick any amusement park, anywhere on the planet, and where are the longest, most aggravating lines? The roller coasters, of course! They are the main attractions these days, with millions strapping themselves into scream machines because they love being scared in a safe environment. The success of a ride can easily be measured in smiles and screams.

Would You Like to Know More About Roller Coaster Design?

Have you ever wondered what it takes to design and build a roller coaster? At last, there's a book that shows you. A mix of engineering and art, roller coasters are complex three-dimensional puzzles consisting of thousands of individual parts. Designers spend countless hours creating and tweaking ride paths to push the envelope of exhilaration, all while maintaining the highest safety standards. *Coasters 101: An Engineering Guide to Roller Coaster Design* examines the numerous diverse aspects of roller coaster engineering, including some of the mathematical formulas and engineering concepts used.

A few of the topics covered include:

Design Software and Computer Technology
Project Management
Wheel Design and Material Selection
Track Fabrication Techniques
Daily Inspections and Preventive Maintenance
Amusement Industry Safety Standards
Career Advice
And much more!

This technical guide is the most detailed roller coaster design book to date and will take you through the entire process, from concept to creation. A must read for every enthusiast and aspiring roller coaster engineer!

Get **Coasters 101: An Engineering Guide to Roller Coaster Design** from Amazon.com today.

Did You Like The 50 Most Terrifying Roller Coasters Ever Built?

Before you go, I'd like to say "thank you" for purchasing my book. I know you could have picked from dozens of other books but you took a chance on mine. So a big thanks for ordering this book and reading all the way to the end.

Now I'd like to ask for a *small* favor. Could you please take a minute or two and leave a review for this book on Amazon.com? Your comments are really valuable because they will guide future editions of this book and I'm always striving to improve my writing.

About the Author

Nick Weisenberger is the author of *Coasters 101: An Engineer's Guide to Roller Coaster Design*, an in-depth look at how a roller coaster is designed, from concept through construction. Nick is currently co-manager of Coaster101.com as well as a member of the ASTM International F-24 committee on Amusement Rides and Devices. He's ridden over one hundred and fifty different coasters and in August 2009, he participated in the Coasting for Kids Ride-a-thon where he endured a ten hour marathon ride (that's 105 laps) and helped raise over $10,000 for Give Kids the World charity. An avid traveler, look for Nick on the midways of your local amusement park!

What to know more? Drop by and check out Coaster101.com, a growing resource and community for roller coaster enthusiasts, aspiring students, and theme park fans.

Questions or comments? Email me:
nick@coaster101.com

Or feel free to say hi on Twitter (@NTWProductions).

Other Works by Nick Weisenberger

Coasters 101: An Engineer's Guide to Roller Coaster Design

The 50 Most *Terrifying* Roller Coasters Ever Built

The 50 Most *Unique* Roller Coasters Ever Built

Things to Do in the Smokies with Kids

Once I was Adopted

Appendix I: Glossary

4th Dimension: Controlled rotatable seats cantilevered on each side of the track.

Airtime: Roller coasters can thrust negative Gs on riders causing them to momentarily lift off their seats and become "weightless." As the vehicle flies over the top of a hill the load on the passenger becomes less than Earth's gravity and, in the extreme, could throw an unrestrained passenger out of the car. Scream machines with oodles of so-called "airtime" moments or "butterflies in your stomach" thrills rank among the world's best. Negative g-forces cannot be too great because when under high negative g forces blood rushed to the head and can cause "red out."

Block: A block is a section of a roller coaster's track with a controllable start and stop point. Only one train may occupy a block at a time.

Bobsled: Cars travel freely down a U-shaped track (no rails) like a bobsled except on wheels.

Bunny Hops: A series of small hills engineered to give repeated doses of airtime

Cobra roll: A half-loop followed by half a corkscrew, then another half corkscrew into another half-loop. The trains are inverted twice and exit the element the opposite direction in which they entered.

Corkscrew: A loop where the entrance and exit points have been stretched apart.

Cycle: When the train completes one circuit around the course. When trains are run continuously this is called cycling.

Dark ride: An indoor ride, usually slow moving through sets based on a central theme, sometime will feature interactivity like shooting at targets

Dive loop: The track twists upward and to the side, similar to half a corkscrew, before diving towards the ground in a half-loop. Basically, the opposite of an Immelman inversion.

Dueling: Two separate tracks but mostly not parallel. Usually contain several head-on, near miss collision sensations.

Floorless: The vehicle sits above the track but contains no floor between the rider's feet and the rails, allowing their legs to dangle freely.

G-force: G-force is expressed as a ratio of the force developed in changing speed or direction relative to the force felt due to the Earth's gravity. The smaller the curve radius and the higher the speed, the greater the g-force felt. Thus, a 2g force on a 100 pound body causes it to weigh 200 pounds (Weight = Mass x G-force). Indianapolis 500 racers are subjected to more than 3g's in the corners of their hairpin turns while there are looping coasters that subject passengers to as much as 6g's. Positive g-forces, meaning those that push your butt into the seat, become uncomfortable for the human body at +5g and may cause the loss of consciousness.

Giga coaster: Any roller coaster with at least one element between 300 and 399 feet tall.

Hyper coaster: Any roller coaster with at least one element between 200 and 299 feet tall.

Imagineer: A person who works for Walt Disney Imagineering. This word is a combination of engineer and imagination.

Immelman: Named after the aircraft maneuver pioneered by Max Immelman, the inversion begins with a vertical loop but at the apex of the inversion turns into a corkscrew exiting at the side instead of completing the loop. The opposite of a dive loop element.

Inversion: An element on a roller coaster track which

turns riders 180 degrees upside down and then rights them again, such as a loop, corkscrew, or barrel roll (among others).

Inverted: Vehicle is fixed below the rails with rider's feet hanging freely and is able to invert upside down.

Laydown/Flying: Riders are parallel to the rails, either on their back or stomach.

Mobius: A racing or dueling roller coaster with one continuous track instead of two separate ones.

Motorbike: Riders straddle the seats as if riding a motorcycle, jet ski, or horse.

Pipeline: Riders are positioned between the rails instead of above or below them.

Queue: A line you stand in for an attraction, food, or entry/exit.

Racing Coaster: Two separate tracks usually parallel for most of the course. Trains are released simultaneously so they race from start to finish.

Sit down: Traditional roller coaster with vehicles above the rails.

Spinning: Seats can freely spin on a horizontal axis.

Standup: Riders are restrained in a standing position.

Swinging suspended: The vehicle hangs below the rails and can freely swing from side to side but does not invert.

Themed: The central idea or concept for an attraction or area.

THRC: Theoretical Hourly Ride Capacity is the number of guests per hour that can experience an attraction under optimal operating conditions. Calculated by: Riders per bench*benches per car*cars per train*(60min/ride time minutes).

Wingrider: The seats are fixed on both sides of the vehicle outside of the rails.

Appendix II: Acronyms

The following is a list of acronyms found within this text and includes common terms used throughout the amusement industry (in alphabetical order).

ACE: American Coaster Enthusiasts
ARB: Anti-Roll Back
ASTM: American Society of Standards and Materials
CAD: Computer Aided Design
FEA: Finite Element Analysis
IAAPA: International Association of Amusement Parks and Attractions
ISO: International Organization for Standardization
LIM: Linear Induction Motor
LOTO: Lock Out Tag Out
LSM: Linear Synchronous Motor
MBD: Model Based Definition
MTBF: Mean Time Between Failures
MTTR: Mean Time To Repair
OEM: Original Equipment Manufacturer
OSS: Operator Safety System
PLC: Programmable Logic Controller
POV: Point of View
RA: Ride Analysis
RAC: Ride Access Control
RCDB: Roller Coaster Data Base
SBNO: Standing But Not Operating
SLC: Suspended Looping Coaster
SRCS: Safety Related Control Systems
T&A: Test and Adjust
THRC: Theoretical Hourly Ride Capacity

Appendix III: Resources

American Coaster Enthusiasts (ACE)
http://www.aceonline.org/

ASTM International
http://www.ASTM.org

Amusement Industry Manufacturers and Suppliers (AIMS)
http://www.aimsintl.org/

Amusement Today
http://amusementtoday.com/
http://www.goldenticketawards.com/

International Association of Amusement Parks and Aquariums (IAAPA)
http://www.IAAPA.org/

Coaster101
http://www.Coaster101.com

Roller Coaster Database
http://www.RCDB.com

Photography Credits

Images Used: Some images were purchased under the license of royalty free stock photography websites. As part of this license, these images cannot be shared, formatter, or modified in any way. Other images are included as part of the Creative Commons License. These sites have been included with full attribution.

Cover image:
Diamondback at Kings Island by Nick Weisenberger

Renderings:
Batman: The Ride and Insane vehicles by Patick McGarvey

Pictures by Nick Weisenberger:
Wicked at Lagoon Park
Flying Turns at Knoebels
Sea Dragon at Jungle Jack's Landing
Millennium Force and Gatekeeper at Cedar Point
Incredible Hulk at Islands of Adventure
Son of Beast at Kings Island
The Voyage at Holiday World

Pictures by John Stevenson:
Hades 360 at Mount Olympus
Goliath at Six Flags Great America

Flickr Pictures distributed under a Cc-BY 2.0 License:
http://creativecommons.org/licenses/by/2.0/

The Rattler by Jon Seidman, https://flic.kr/p/8oZgXG

Riddler's Revenge Ride – Six Flags Magic Mountain by Jeff Turner, https://flic.kr/p/6vKaN8, https://flic.kr/p/6vJF4m

Saw the Ride by LH*Photography, https://flic.kr/p/75BFT3

Nemesis by Jenny Brown, https://flic.kr/p/bXpmuY

Alpengeist by Patrick McGarvey, https://flic.kr/p/7eNiaS

Tower of Terror by Xander Buys, https://flic.kr/p/eT3P4q

Flip Around by Yudis Asnar, https://flic.kr/p/2WX8SM

El Toro by Sarah Ackerman, https://flic.kr/p/fcUBvW

El Toro, Six Flags Great Adventure by hampus, https://flic.kr/p/qwebz8

G-Force at Drayton Manor by Jeremy Thompson, https://flic.kr/p/8fn3DM

Formula Rossa by Sarah Ackerman, https://flic.kr/p/eamLYN

Kingda Ka – Great Adventure by Chun Yip So, https://flic.kr/p/8cizZx

Kingda Ka – tower closeup by Adam Ahmed, https://flic.kr/p/uacRp

Superman: the Escape - Magic Mountain by Konrad Summers, https://flic.kr/p/5noxgN

Made in the USA
Coppell, TX
18 September 2020